Sincerely, America

A Message of Hope

Lauren Riser

Sincerely, America: A Message of Hope

Printed in the United States of America

For permissions or to purchase books in quantity, please contact Lauren D. Riser by email at laurend.riser@gmail.com.

Library of Congress Control Number: 2020915595
ISBN: 978-0-578-74162-8

DEDICATED

To those who have experienced racial injustice
in the name of America and what it stands for.
We see you, we hear you...

WE STAND WITH YOU.

FOREWORD

This is a poetic letter from America to its people about its past and its future. It is a letter about being misguided, figuring out a people's worth, and journeying on the road to redemption. This letter is one of sincerity, empathy, and love. It is a simple truth showing that an apology may not solve every problem, but it needs to be heard to start the healing process. And we, as Americans, need healing.

America, America,
I am the land of the
free and the home of
the brave.

I am here to express
my condolences
for the lives I did
not save.

TOP
ER BY POLICE

For the poetic words said about me that
were not always carried out,

and to the ones who have entrusted me but
whom I have failed miserably, no doubt,

please know…

Believes
MATTER
Atatiana
Jefferson
Walter
Scott

...that I am sorry.

All people of all colors of all backgrounds was my plan,

realizing that among all things, it takes diversity to make me grand.

But somewhere
along my journey,
I got distracted, and
the message was lost.

Just now, I am
understanding that
the ones representing
diversity are paying
the cost.

To my Black brothers and sisters, your trauma, I know, has always been real.

"Black Lives Matter" is such an obvious statement, one that goes without question, one that no man should appeal.

The idea that any race of people inhabiting my lands should have to fight for the notion that they are better alive than dead

serves as a testament today as to why we cannot get ahead.

The fact that racism still exists today is not something that I am proud of.

To actively respect my flag more than my people is a mindset we must get out of.

Indivisibility is what I preach, it is what you pledge, it is how I stand!

Under God, we are indivisible but so easily divided under man.

Liberty and justice for all is a promise, a serious oath that I took

not to a certain race or people of a certain color, although we are living out how that would look.

Mayflower

My name, "America,"
for many, still stands
for great opportunity
otherwise rarely
achievable.

Even those who
landed on me "first"
were seeking freedom
once inconceivable.

The duties of founding fathers
and first comers were to pass on
what they'd learned and earned
to the next generation

to share knowledge and
newfound wisdom with the world,
not to expand and encourage
degradation.

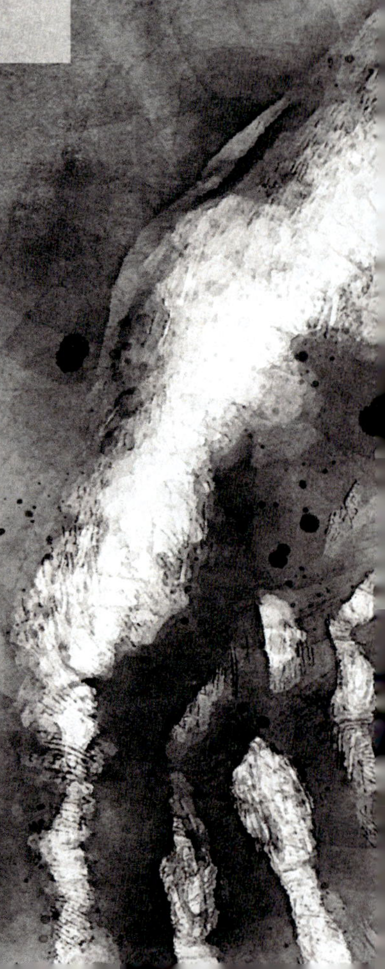

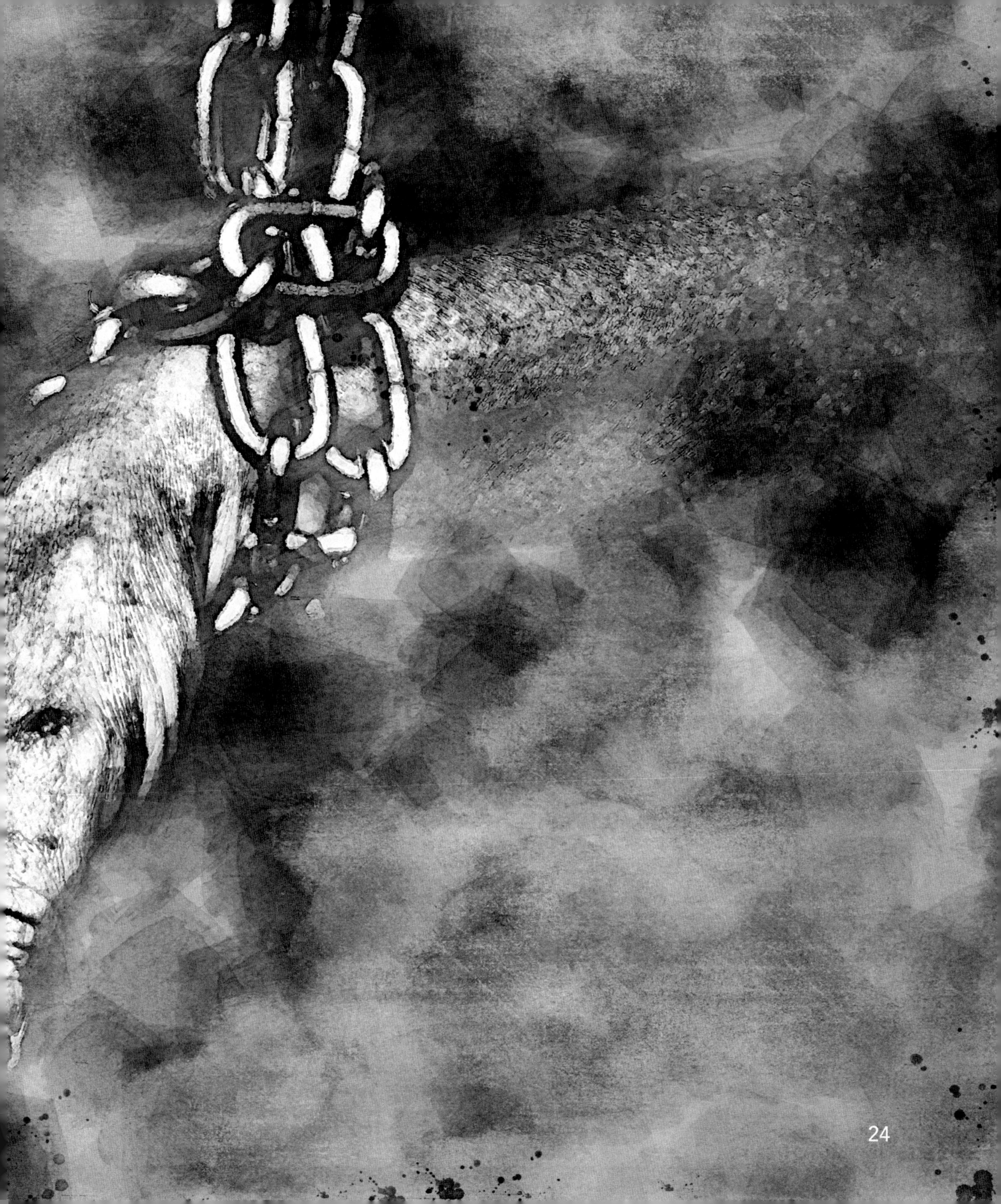

In this time of chaos, in this time of grief, I will step up and shoulder all the blame

for the injustices, for the wrongdoings, and for the hurt that have caused so many pain.

I unapologetically and with urgency shout from the mountain tops,

"THINGS HAVE TO CHANGE!"

No longer is it okay to sit back and allow the inhumane to use my name in vain!

13

From North to South, from East to West, I want all who say my name

to know that what I stand for is real and not just words we sing along to at games.

I know that so
far, my words
may seem ugly;
the truth is not
always attractive.

But I truly have
so much faith
in the rising
generations who
are investing
their time in
being active.

To actively listen, to actively learn, to actively acknowledge is key.

To give your respect to all people of all backgrounds has always been a part of my original decree.

CHICAGO
POLICE

So, from here on out, let us all take a vow to make me great, not AGAIN, but AT LAST,

to continually work together in a positive environment showing lessons learned from our past.

We all are loved, we all hold value, no one being better than the other.

So, when you pass one another in the street or at the store, know that he or she is your sister or your brother.

I will end this
letter hoping
that I have
expressed
myself clearly,
but know my
fate is truly up
to you!

I am very
appreciative
that you have
lent me your
ear to extend
apologies long
overdue.

If you have a minute,
please take the time to share
my letter across this nation.

I know that the truths
that I have spoken and my
apologies are only a fraction
of deserved reparations.

I am just hoping it is a
start to a better life,
a better world, and at
the very least, a more
productive conversation.

Sincerely,
America

My people, you are truly my
greatest assets, my greatest hopes,
my claim to fame. I am begging
you, please, think before you act
in the future and let your actions
accurately represent my name.

Sincerely,
America

GLOSSARY

Achievable: To be able to be achieved. To be possible to succeed.

Acknowledge: To recognize and admit to the fact or being of.

Appeal: To question a thing that has been proven.

Appreciative: To be thankful, to show gratitude.

Assets: Things that hold or contribute value.

Black Lives Matter: A political and social movement emphasizing basic human rights and racial equality for Black people and campaigning against various forms of racism.

Condolences: An expression of empathy towards someone experiencing hardships or sadness.

Decree: A formal and authoritative mandate, one holding the force of law.

Degradation: The act of humiliating and treating someone with no regard.

Diversity: Having many different nationalities, races, kinds, etc. occupying the same space.

Entrusted: To confide in, to trust in.

Environment: The surroundings in which you exist.

Expand: To grow or increase in mass or size.

Extend: To offer or hold out. To stretch out.

Faith: A strong belief in something that one has no proof of.

Fate: An inevitable future.

Founding Fathers: Delegates to the Constitutional Convention in Philadelphia in 1787.

Grand: Large. Something that has a big impact.

Inconceivable: To be unbelievable, unheard of and unthinkable.

Indivisibility: Not being able to divide. Quality of being one in representation.

Inhabiting: The act of living in or to take up residence in.

Inhumane: To lack kindness in action. To be human is kind, and to be inhuman is unkind.

Injustices: Unfair actions or treatment taken against an individual. Violations of someone's rights.

Investing: The act of putting time, money or effort into something for future gain.

Mindset: An attitude or belief one holds towards something.

Notion: One's opinion or belief towards something.

Oath: Words spoken in a way in which a promise is made.

Overdue: Past due, long waited for.

Pledge: A promise to do or not do something.

Positive: A good outlook, one of happiness and good feelings.

Productive: The act of producing. Getting things done.

Racism: A belief that inherent differences among various human racial groups determine cultural achievement, usually involving the idea that one's own race is superior and has the right to dominate others or that a particular racial group is inferior to the others.

Reparations: To make amends for wrongdoings that have transpired.

Representing: Standing in place of.

Respect: To show consideration for.

Testament: A proof of or witness of something.

Trauma: An experience that causes mental and physical pain.

Unapologetically: Not expressing fault or wrongdoing.

Vain: Having no real significance. Worthless.

Value: Showing worth.

Vow: A promise or commitment.

ABOUT THE AUTHOR

Lauren Riser is an author, among her multitude of other talents. She is a native of Carrollton, Texas, and lives with her husband, Jay, in a lively household that includes two daughters, two sons, a lot of fun, and a true spirit of love.

Made in the USA
Monee, IL
14 October 2020

44490473R00036